IF PREHISTORIC BEASTS WERE ALIVE TODAY

by Matthew Rake

Illustrated by Simon Mendez

Beetle Books and Hungry Banana are imprints of Hungry Tomato

First published 2019
by Hungry Tomato Ltd
F1, Old Barkery Studios
Blewetts Wharf
Malpas Road
Truro, TR1 1JQ,
United Kingdom

A CIP catalogue record for this book is available from the British Library.

US edition (Beetle Books)
ISBN 978-1-913077-136

UK edition (Hungry Banana)
ISBN 978-1-910684-276

Discover more at
www.mybeetlebooks.com
www.hungrytomato.com

CONTENTS

*mya = million years ago

THE BIG, THE BAD, AND THE UGLY

Everyone knows about the dinosaurs and how scary some of them were. But did you know there were lots of other equally savage prehistoric creatures? How about the crocodile that liked to dine on dinosaurs? Or the bird that stood 8 feet (2.5 m) tall and used its 18-inch (46-cm) beak like a hatchet? Now can you imagine what might happen if they appeared in today's world? Well, you are about to find out . . .

All life started in the sea—and that's where the first animals evolved, around 550 million years ago. Some were pretty weird, such as 2.5-in. (6-cm) *Opabinia* (right) with its five eyes and long grasping claw at the end of a long, hose-like arm.

Pretty soon, animals became ferocious. About 475 million years ago, there were massive predators such as sea scorpions and shelled creatures, called nautiloids, as large as crocodiles. Eventually, some sea animals evolved limbs and hauled themselves on to land. One was *Acanthostega* (below), though it probably still kept close to water.

Opabinia

Acanthostega

Reptiles were the first animals with backbones to live only on land. Some grew to an enormous size, like the fearsome *Sarcosuchus* (see page 32). Some evolved leathery wings and took to the skies. One of the first flying reptiles, or pterosaurs, was *Eudimorphodon* (below). **The largest was Quetzalcoatlus (see page 38), which hunted or scavenged on land.**

Eudimorphodon

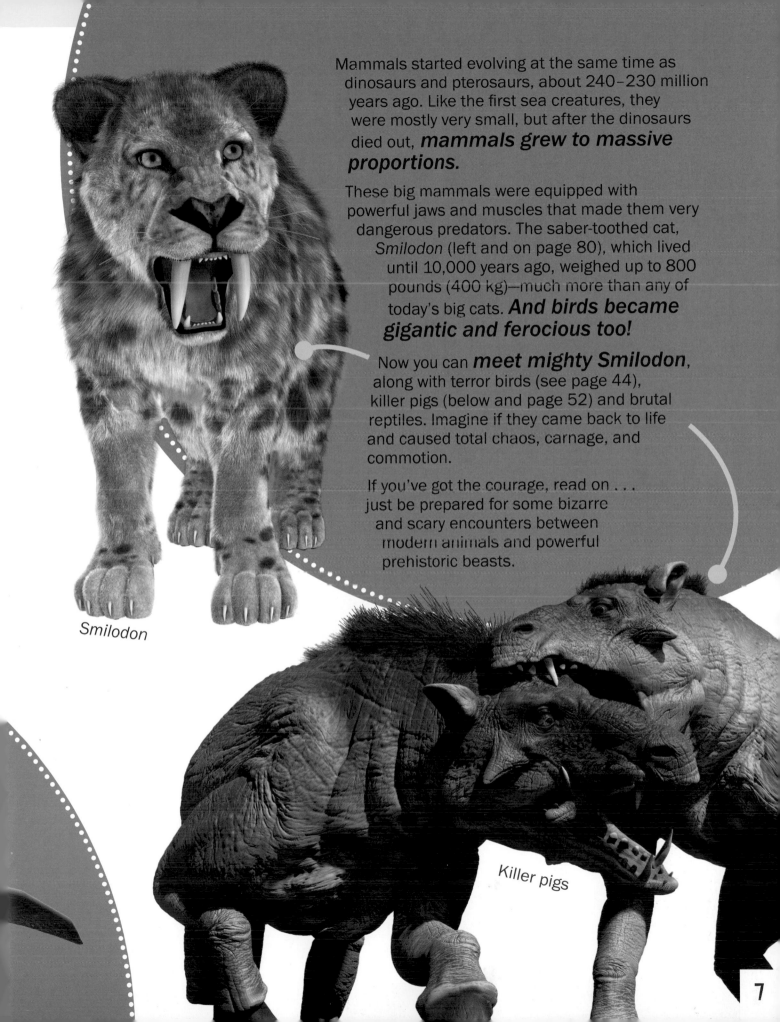

Mammals started evolving at the same time as dinosaurs and pterosaurs, about 240–230 million years ago. Like the first sea creatures, they were mostly very small, but after the dinosaurs died out, **mammals grew to massive proportions.**

These big mammals were equipped with powerful jaws and muscles that made them very dangerous predators. The saber-toothed cat, *Smilodon* (left and on page 80), which lived until 10,000 years ago, weighed up to 800 pounds (400 kg)—much more than any of today's big cats. **And birds became gigantic and ferocious too!**

Now you can **meet mighty Smilodon**, along with terror birds (see page 44), killer pigs (below and page 52) and brutal reptiles. Imagine if they came back to life and caused total chaos, carnage, and commotion.

If you've got the courage, read on . . . just be prepared for some bizarre and scary encounters between modern animals and powerful prehistoric beasts.

Smilodon

Killer pigs

TENTACLED TERROR
CAMEROCERAS

Modern nautiloids swim in the seas around Australia and the Philippines. They live in shells, look pretty, and are only about 8 in. (20 cm) long. They certainly can't do any harm to a sizeable creature. Well, check out this nautiloid—it's called *Cameroceras*. It's longer than your average minivan, and it's a ruthless predator—as this crocodile would surely admit.

Cameroceras is using its tangle of grasping tentacles to drag its prey towards its beak. And you wouldn't want to go anywhere near the beak. It can crunch straight through hard shells—so the armored scales of this small crocodile aren't going to give it too much trouble. And worse is to come. Modern nautiloids have a toothed tongue known as a radula. This allows them to scrape and cut out the soft, fleshy parts of its victim. Scientists think *Cameroceras* would have had exactly the same tongue. Imagine if *Cameroceras* lived alongside today's sea creatures. It's hard to pity a vicious creature like a crocodile, but in this case, perhaps it deserves a little sympathy.

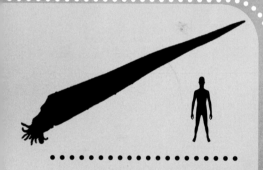

CAMEROCERAS
PRONOUNCED
Cam-eh-RO-seh-rass

LIVED
Northern seas,
470–451 million
years ago

LENGTH
Up to 20 feet (6 m)

HEAVILY ARMED

Modern nautiloids have up to 94 tentacles. Why do they need so many? Some tentacles are used to touch and sense chemicals. Some bring food to its beak. These ones are coated with a sticky substance to help the food stay on!

9

BIG NIPPER
SEA SCORPION OR EURYPTERID

Let's face it, we are all a little frightened of scorpions—even though they are only a few centimetres long. Can you imagine scorpions bigger than an adult human? No? Well, meet the modern scorpion's bigger, badder prehistoric ancestors: the sea scorpions or eurypterids. They swam through ancient oceans and scuttled across sea floors, terrorizing every other living thing they came in contact with.

The sea scorpion chased down prey quickly with the help of its long tail and paddle-like swimming legs. Then it would go in for the kill with its huge claws. These were the size of tennis rackets and covered with deadly spines, perfect for holding the unfortunate victim against the sea floor and then slicing and shredding it! The only thing it was missing was an underwater cutting board.

What if sea scorpions lived today? You'd have to feel sorry for the diver here. But if he's a strong swimmer, he'd probably lose no more than a flipper.

EURYPTERID
PRONOUNCED
You-RIP-ter-id

LIVED
Seas worldwide, around 467–250 million years ago

LENGTH
Up to 8 feet (2.5 m)

FOSSIL FINDS

What's New York famous for? Yeah, a city full of skyscrapers, Broadway theaters, and Fifth Avenue shops. But New York state has one big claim to fame: hundreds of eurypterid finds, including the first one ever, in 1818. In fact, the sea scorpion is the designated state fossil.

PART BEAST, PART BATTLESHIP
DUNKLEOSTEUS

This dolphin might look as if it is getting away from the huge, superpowerful fish, *Dunkleosteus*. But *Dunkleosteus* does not actually have to catch the dolphin. All it needs to do is get close enough to open its mouth. It can do this in one-fiftieth of a second—so quickly that it would create a suction force to pull the dolphin backwards into its mouth. And once it has its prey in its jaws, there is no hope. *Dunkleosteus*'s bite force has been estimated at 1,100 pounds (5,000 Newtons)—that's more powerful than the bite of a lion, tiger, or hyena!

Not surprisingly, *Dunkleosteus* was an apex predator in its time—this means that no other creature preyed upon it. However, *Dunkleosteus* did have to watch out for one other animal—fellow *Dunkleosteus*. Some fossils show injuries created by the razor-sharp plating of other *Dunkleosteus*. Maybe they fought over territory—or, more likely, they were simply trying to eat each other.

DUNKLEOSTEUS

PRONOUNCED
Dun-kul-OSS-tee-us

LIVED
Shallow seas worldwide, 380–360 million years ago

LENGTH
Up to 10 m (33 ft)

WEIGHT
3–4 tonnes (3.3–4.4 US tons)

ARMOR-PLATED

Dunkleosteus was one of a group of armored fish known as placoderms, which means "plate-skinned" in Greek. Its skull was about 4 feet (1.3 m) wide and had armor-plating all around it. The plating was up to 2 inches (5 cm) thick, but at the jaws, this thinned down to razor-sharp edges. These made perfect blades for crushing fish.

SHAKE A LEG
ARTHROPLEURA

Can you imagine coming home after a long day to be greeted by two alligator-sized millipede? The millipedes, which seem to have made themselves at home, are *Arthropleura*. They lived in the Carboniferous period more than 300 million years ago. Scientists think they grew so big because there was lots of oxygen in the atmosphere. There were also no big predators living on land for *Arthropleura* to deal with. (The big predators were all in the sea!)

Scientists aren't completely sure what these giants ate. If *Arthropleura* had been a carnivore, it would have needed strong, hard mouthparts, and these fossilize well. But none have ever been found, and scientists think it was probably a herbivore.

So whoever lives in this house need not be too alarmed. The *Arthropleura* aren't after them—the bizarre visitors probably just want a quick munch at the fruit bowl or the house plants!

ARTHROPLEURA
PRONOUNCED
Ar-throw-PLOO-rah

LIVED
Eastern North America and Western Europe, 355–300 million years ago

LENGTH
Up to 7 feet 6 inches (2.3 m)

END TO END
The biggest millipedes of today, such as *Archispirostreptus gigas* of East Africa, reach only around 12 inches (30 cm) long. You would need to put seven or eight of these end to end to match the length of *Arthropleura*.

STRETCH YOUR LEGS
Like many modern millipedes, *Arthropleura* might have eaten dead plant matter. So maybe these two should see if there's a compost heap in the garden. It would be a chance for them to stretch their legs—all 40 of them!

DEADLY DRAGONFLY
MEGANEURA

To you, dragonflies might seem like small, frail creatures. But to insects, they are pretty ruthless hunters. Midges and mosquitoes, butterflies and moths, mayflies and damselflies all end up as dinner for dragonflies.

Dragonflies hunt on the wing, using their sharp eyesight and strong flying skills to chase down their prey. To kill, the dragonfly usually bites its victim on the head then carries it in its legs to a perch where it will remove the wings and eat the prey, head first.

Luckily, dragonflies in Europe and North America are only 3 inches (8 cm) long, with a 4.7-inch (12-cm) wingspan. But what if they had the wingspan of a small hawk? Well, meet *Meganeura*, the giant dragonfly that lived in the Carboniferous period 300 million years ago. Like modern dragonflies, it probably ate insects, but, given its massive size, it may also have had a taste for small amphibians, millipedes, centipedes, and even the odd reptile. These days it would have even more choice, including small mammals like this rat—whose future isn't looking too good right about now!

MEGANEURA
PRONOUNCED
Meg-ah-NEW-rah
LIVED
Western Europe,
300 million
years ago
WINGSPAN
25.6–30 inches (65–
75 cm)

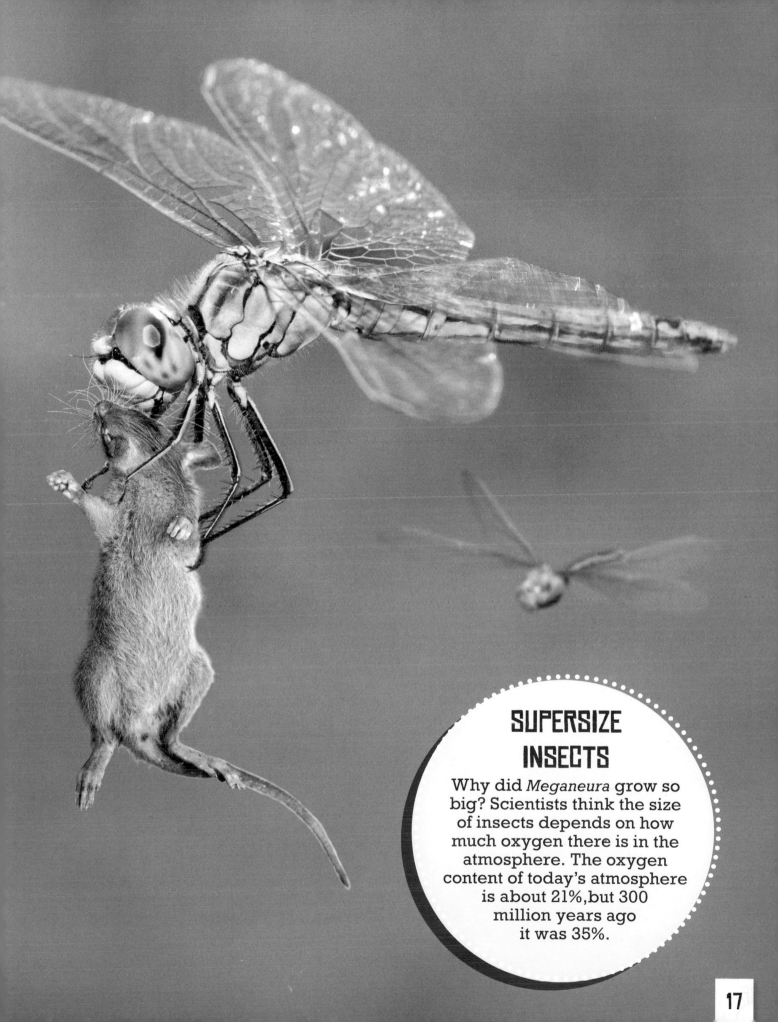

SUPERSIZE INSECTS

Why did *Meganeura* grow so big? Scientists think the size of insects depends on how much oxygen there is in the atmosphere. The oxygen content of today's atmosphere is about 21%, but 300 million years ago it was 35%.

ROCKING THE BOAT
DIMETRODON

Er, there appears to be a rather unexpected entrant in this year's yacht race. It has a sail but it doesn't look interested in the race. In fact, it seems to be going after the sailors, not the first prize. This curious creature is *Dimetrodon,* and why it had a sail on its back is a mystery. It was certainly not to help it glide across the water—although that was one of the theories when this reptile-like creature was first discovered in the 19th century. Another theory was that it might swim on its back and use the sail like a fin! Other people thought the sail camouflaged the animal among reeds as it waited for prey—though a better way of concealing yourself might be not having one at all!

For this capsized yachtsman, *Dimetrodon*'s sail should be the last thing on his mind—it's the teeth he should be worried about. *Dimetrodon* was one of the first animals to have serrated teeth perfect for slicing through flesh . . .

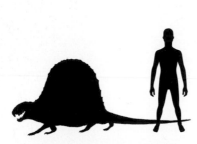

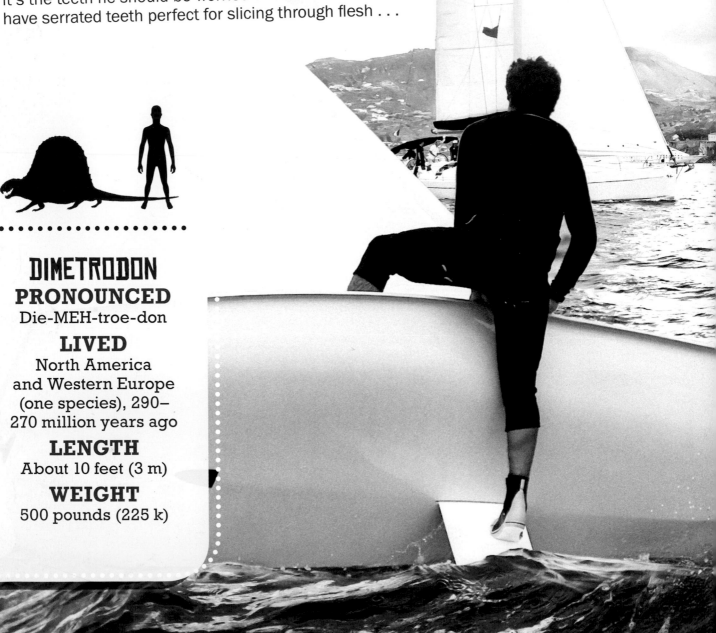

DIMETRODON
PRONOUNCED
Die-MEH-troe-don

LIVED
North America and Western Europe (one species), 290–270 million years ago

LENGTH
About 10 feet (3 m)

WEIGHT
500 pounds (225 k)

WARMING UP

Experts now think the sail might have controlled *Dimetrodon*'s body temperature. Just as cold-blooded reptiles need to warm up in the morning, maybe the sail helped *Dimetrodon* soak up sunshine. Or perhaps, like the peacock's tail, it was a way of attracting mates—and the male *Dimetrodon* did have a bigger sail than the female!

EUROPEAN SPECIES

So far scientists have found 13 species of *Dimetrodon*. The first one was discovered in 1878. The latest discovery, *Dimetrodon teutonis*, found in 2001 in Germany, is the only species to have been found in Europe.

HORNED HORROR
ESTEMMENOSUCHUS

So what on Earth is this crazy-looking creature? Is it a rhino? A hippo? A combination of the two? No, it's an *Estemmenosuchus*. And it's not some sort of dinosaur either—this mammal-like reptile lived about 25 million years before the first dinosaurs came along.

Don't worry—if *Estemmenosuchus* looks like a confusing creature to you, it is for scientists, too. They can't work out whether it was a carnivore (meat-eater) or a herbivore (plant-eater). Its sharp canine and incisor teeth look as if they were made for ripping into flesh. But its big body seems made for digesting plant matter. And its short, widely set front legs are perfect for lowering its head to the ground to graze on plants. Maybe it's an omnivore, meaning it ate both meat and plants.

Whatever the answer, it doesn't look as if it will back down in this stand off with a lion. It might not be the speediest of animals, but with its huge horns and beefy body, it can probably look after itself. Its skull alone, at 26 inches (65 cm), is twice the length of the lion's. The king of the jungle might just have a rival for its crown.

ESTEMMENOSUCHUS

PRONOUNCED
Ess-tim-en-oh-SUE-kuss

LIVED
Russia, about 267 million years ago

LENGTH
Up to 15 feet (4.5 m)

WEIGHT
About 990 pounds (450 kg)

HEY, GOOD-LOOKIN'

The horns of *Estemmenosuchus* grew up and out from the skull bones and were probably designed for attracting mates, just as a peacock's feathers attract peahens.

HEAD-BUTTING BEAST
MOSCHOPS

These days, there are people who earn money by walking dogs. It sounds like a nice job, with lots of fresh air and exercise. But surely this dog walker should be getting paid extra? After all, look at that beast she has to deal with. It's a *Moschops*, a massive mammal-like reptile that lived before the age of the dinosaurs. And, with a big, barrel-shaped body on top of those short legs, it doesn't look as if it wants to go anywhere fast.

Trying to encourage it to get a move on might not be the wisest thing. *Moschops'* skull was up to 4 inches (10 cm) thick—that's the width of a brick! It used it to head-butt rival *Moschops*, and some scientists even think they got on their hind legs to fight, like sumo wrestlers. So if this *Moschops* wants to go at its own pace, the dog walker should let it!

MOSCHOPS
PRONOUNCED
MOSS-chops

LIVED
Forests of
South Africa,
267–260 million
years ago

LENGTH
About 9 feet (2.7 m)

WEIGHT
About 2,000 pounds
(914 kg)

TV STAR

In the 1980s, a *Moschops* was the star of an animated TV series of that name. The show also featured his friend Ally, an *Allosaurus*, grandfather *Diplodocus,* and Uncle Rex (yes, a *T. rex*). It wasn't exactly accurate. All those animals actually lived millions and millions of years apart!

RUTHLESS REPTILE
INOSTRANCEVIA

Wolves are very territorial—they roam over many miles, defending their range by howling and scent-marking. But more strong-arm tactics will be necessary to tackle this impostor. It's *Inostrancevia*, which had lethal canine teeth up to 6 inches (15 cm) long in its upper jaw. Its back teeth were tiny in comparison, but this didn't matter because *Inostrancevia* didn't chew its food. It simply ripped open prey and swallowed large chunks of meat. Its lower jaw was hinged so it could open its mouth very wide. One of the cubs might be swallowed whole if it really wanted to wolf down its meal.

Inostrancevia lived before the age of the dinosaurs. It was a reptile but belonged to the therapsid group from which mammals evolved. Reptiles generally have sprawling limbs, but *Inostrancevia* had a more upright posture. Compared to other animals of the time, it was a good runner as its legs were long relative to the size of its body. But it is not going to outpace these wolves—they can run for 30 miles (48 km) a day. For this *Inostrancevia*, it's not a question of fight or flight. It's just fight . . .

INOSTRANCEVIA
PRONOUNCED
In-oh-stran-SEE-vee-ah

LIVED
Northern Russia,
260–254 million
years ago

LENGTH
up to 11 feet 6 inches
(3.5 m); skull: up to
24 inches (60 cm) long

Inostrancevia is known as a gorgonopsian reptile. This order of reptiles had many mammal-like features, including different-shaped teeth, well-developed ear bones, and upright legs. But they are not thought to have had fur like mammals.

STRETCH-NECKED SAVAGE
TANYSTROPHEUS

Who needs a fishing rod when you have a neck 10 feet (3 m) long? This is *Tanystropheus,* and modern scientists believe its super-stretched neck helped it to catch fish. However, when Italian palaeontologist Francesco Bassani first discovered *Tanystropheus* fossils in 1886, he couldn't believe any animal could have such a long neck. So he decided he must have found the wing bones of a giant pterosaur—a flying reptile that lived during the days of the dinosaurs.

Although we now know *Tanystropheus* definitely didn't fly, we are still not sure whether it lived in water or on land. Scientists now think it probably lived somewhere in between—near the shoreline. Its front legs are shorter than the back ones, which would have been perfect for leaning forward at the water's edge for feeding. It probably liked to feed at tidal pools, which would be restocked with new fish every time the tide came in. But it might have taken a dip in the sea if it saw some particularly juicy prey. Good thing *Tanystropheus* isn't around today to catch dogs going for a swim!

TANYSTROPHEUS
PRONOUNCED
Tan-ee-STROH-fee-us

LIVED
Shores of Europe,
215 million years ago

LENGTH
About 20 feet (6 m)

WEIGHT
300 pounds (140 kg)

TALL TAIL

Tanystropheus' neck was about 10 feet (3 m), or half its total length. Its tail was almost 6 ft 6 in (2 m) long, a third of its length. But its body was only about 3 ft 3 in (1 m) long, just one-sixth of its length.

BIG MOUTH
LEEDSICHTHYS

This fish might look terrifying, and it did have 40,000 teeth, but it wasn't a predatory animal. Like today's blue whale, *Leedsichthys* lived on zooplankton: tiny animals, including shrimp, fish, and jellyfish, that float near the surface of the sea. To get as much zooplankton as possible, *Leedsichthys* opened its mouth wide, and only used the teeth to filter out the zooplankton from sea water. Still, these kids want to watch out—that mouth is over 6 feet 6 inches (2 m) wide, and they don't want to end up with the zooplankton!

Unfortunately, lots about *Leedsichthys* remains mysterious, and scientists have continually changed their minds about how big it is. At the start of the 20th century, they thought it was 30 feet (9 m) long. But by the end of the century, they estimated it was more than 100 feet (30 m). Now it has been downsized to 54 feet (16.5 m). It won't surprise you that the Latin name of this creature is *Leedsichthys problematicus*. It has proved very problematicus indeed. But one thing is for certain, it is the biggest bony fish ever discovered. (*Megalodon* was bigger, but sharks have skeletons of cartilage, not bone, so are not classified as bony fish).

LEEDSICHTHYS
PRONOUNCED
Leeds-ICK-thiss

LIVED
European and
South American seas,
165–155 million
years ago

LENGTH
up to 54 feet (16.5 m)

FACT TITLE

British farmer Alfred Nicholson Leeds first discovered *Leedsichthys* bones in a pit near Peterborough, England, in 1886. He soon discovered more fossils and started a profitable side business selling them to collectors and museums.

LET'S GET FUNKEI
PLIOSAURUS FUNKEI

Check out this monster erupting out of the sea with a humpback whale in its jaws. This big bruiser of a reptile is *Pliosaurus funkei*. It lived at the time of the dinosaurs, and you could call it the *Tyrannosaurus rex* of the seas. It measured up to 43 feet (13 m)—about the same length as your average bus. Its skull alone was bigger than a human, and it contained teeth as long as carving knives.

Scientists think that most of the time *Pliosaurus funkei* cruised around just using its two front flippers. But for a torpedo-like assault like this, it also used its back flippers to gain extra speed and propel itself towards its giant prey. Of course, these days humpback whales have nothing to fear from any such random attacks—luckily for these peace-loving giants.

PLIOSAURUS FUNKEI
PRONOUNCED
Plio-SORE-us-FUNK-eye

LIVED
Arctic Ocean,
150 million years ago

LENGTH
33–43 ft (10–13 m),
skull: 6 ft 6 in–8 ft
(2–2.5 m)

WEIGHT
25.4 tons(22.3 metric tons)

BIG PREY HUNTERS

Pliosaurs, with their massive jaws and teeth around 12 inches (30 cm) long, evolved to capture large prey including other pliosaurs, plesiosaurs (see page 36) and possibly giant fish such as *Leedsichthys* (see page 28).

3D JIGSAW

Scientists only discovered *Pliosaurus funkei* in 2006. That's when a huge pliosaur skeleton was found on the Arctic islands of Svalbard, Norway. At first, scientists couldn't tell what it was and called it "Predator X." There were around 20,000 fossil pieces, and putting it together was like doing a gigantic 3D jigsaw. Eventually, in 2012, they announced they had found the biggest pliosaur of all time, naming it *Pliosaurus funkei*.

COLD-BLOODED KILLER
SARCOSUCHUS

There has been major disruption on the subway today. But finally something is emerging from the tunnel. Arriving now on platform 1 is, er . . . a crocodile. And not just any croc. This is *Sarcosuchus*—in the days of the dinosaurs, it used to lie in wait in rivers. And even the deadliest dinos needed to be extra careful. *Sarcosuchus* was the length of a bus, weighed more than an elephant, and had more than 100 teeth, including bone-crushing incisors. For protection, it was covered head to tail with scutes: hard plates covered with horn. Basically, it had its own personal suit of armor.

It was also a pretty cunning predator. Like today's crocodiles, *Sarcosuchus* probably waited submerged in the shallows, with its eyes just above the water. In this position, it could look around without moving its head. Unsuspecting dinosaurs that came down for a drink would end up as dinner. So a word of advice for the commuters here: "Stand back from the platform edge—there is a *Sarcosuchus* approaching!"

SARCOSUCHUS
PRONOUNCED

Sark-oh-SUE-kuss

LIVED
Africa and
South America,
112 million years ago

LENGTH
39 feet (12 m);
skull length:
6 feet (1.8 m)

WEIGHT
8.8 tons (8 metric tons)

TOP THAT
The biggest modern crocodile ever measured was Lolong, which lived in captivity in the Philippines. It was 20 ft 3 in (6.17 m) long and weighed 1.18 tons (1.075 metric tons). *Sarcosuchus* was about eight times heavier and twice as long.

EPIC FIGHTS?
Sarcosuchus lived in what is now the Sahara in North Africa. Back then, it wasn't a desert but a lush, tropical region with lots of rivers. *Spinosaurus*, the biggest meat-eating dinosaur ever, also lived there. It's likely the two creatures had epic fights together.

SUPER SNAPPER
XIPHACTINUS

Xiphactinus terrorized the seas at the end of the dinosaur era. Even though it wasn't the biggest marine animal, it was a great predator. So what did it have that other sea beasts didn't? First, with its powerful tail and wing-like fins, it was fast. With a top speed of about 37 miles (60 km) per hour, *Xiphactinus* could swim towards prey—or away from predators— quicker than virtually anything else in the ocean at the time. Second, it had vicious, needle-like teeth, 2.3 inches (6 cm) long and perfect for piercing scales and flesh.

However, it could not chew or slice off smaller pieces, so it ate fish whole. There are lots of fossils to prove this. Inside a 13-foot (4-m) fossil found in 1952 by Walter Sorensen in Kansas, there is a perfectly preserved 6-foot (1.8-m) *Gillicus* fish. Scientists think the *Gillicus*, in a desperate attempt to escape, ripped open the *Xiphactinus*'s stomach and damaged some of its vital organs.

So this *Xiphactinus* better watch out for the swordfish. Let's face it, it doesn't want that sword-like bill flailing around in its stomach.

XIPHACTINUS
PRONOUNCED
Zih-fak-TIE-nuss

LIVED
Seas around
North America,
Europe, Australia,
100–66 million
years ago
LENGTH
13–20 feet (4–6 m)

UNDER WATER

Many *Xiphactinus* fossils have been found in Kansas. So how did lots of fish fossils end up in the middle of the US? When *Xiphactinus* lived, the prehistoric Western Interior Seaway covered much of what is now North America.

COMPLETE SKELETON

The Rocky Mountain Dinosaur Resource Center in Colorado is home to the biggest complete *Xiphactinus* skeleton. It measures 18 ft 4 in (5.6 m), and it took three experts three years to assemble.

STICKING ITS NECK OUT
ELASMOSAURUS

This magnificent beast is really going the extra mile, isn't it? It's an *Elasmosaurus*, a member of the plesiosaur family of marine reptiles that lived from 200 million to around 66 million years ago. It has been described as "a snake threaded through the shell of a turtle," but it certainly didn't have a shell. Its neck alone was about 23 feet (7 m) long, half the length of its entire body.

Scientists think it spent most of its time in the depths, so its heavy neck was buoyed up by the water. To eat, *Elasmosaurus* would swim up to a shoal of fish, probably from below to remain hidden, and then dart its head into the shoal to snatch the fish. Its teeth were sharp and overlapped so that fish could not wriggle free. Then the prey would be swallowed whole and begin the long journey down *Elasmosaurus*'s neck.

The surfer here is probably not in too much danger, though. *Elasmosaurus*' teeth weren't designed for ripping into large prey. It's probably just coming up for air—or to find out what this alien creature is doing floating around on a piece of wood.

ELASMOSAURUS
PRONOUNCED
El-azz-mo-SORE-us

LIVED
North America,
80.5 million
years ago

LENGTH
Up to about
49 feet (15 m)

WEIGHT
2.2 tons (2 metric tons)

A BIT OF A BONEHEAD

US scientist Edward Drinker Cope named the *Elasmosaurus* in 1868. Unfortunately, when he put the skeleton together, he placed the head on the tail! By getting the skull the wrong way round, the professor proved to be a bit of a bonehead himself. *Elasmosaurus* looks rather like *Tanystropheus* on page 26. But it lived about 125 million years later. and was a much bigger and more terrifying creature.

SOARING PTEROSAUR
QUETZALCOATLUS

Okay, at a watering hole, you expect giraffes. But what about the other creatures? They are *Quetzalcoatlus* and have flown in for a quick feed. They're gobbling up the small lizards, amphibians, and mammals that live around streams and lakes.

Quetzalcoatlus was a pterosaur, a type of flying reptile. Pterosaurs evolved 230 million years ago or earlier, about the same time as the dinosaurs. And just like dinosaurs, they got bigger and bigger. *Quetzalcoatlus* lived some 72–66 million years ago and was the biggest pterosaur of all. And if you think it looks big on the ground, imagine it in flight. It is the largest flying creature ever, with a wingspan as wide as a fighter jet.

One thing, however, is a little mystifying: how did this creature get in the air? Some scientists think it jumped from a cliff or used a downward slope as a runway. Others think it vaulted into the air from all fours in what they call a "quad jump!" If so, those giraffes had better get away before they're knocked out by those giant wings . . .

QUETZALCOATLUS
PRONOUNCED
Kwet-ZAL-co-AT-luss

LIVED
North America,
72–66 million
years ago

LENGTH
About 33–36 feet
(10–11 m)

WEIGHT
About 440–550 lb
(200–250 kg)

UP AND AWAY

One study in 2012 found that *Quetzalcoatlus* could fly at 80 miles (130 km) per hour for 7 to 10 days at altitudes of 15,000 ft (4,570 m). Its maximum range was probably about 8,000–12,000 miles (12,800–19,000 km).

DOG VERSUS FROG

BEELZEBUFO

Watch out, there's a *Beelzebufo* about! And it doesn't look like it's in a good mood. This amphibian, also known as the giant devil frog, was the size of a beach ball and lived at the time of the dinosaurs. It was probably a nasty sit-and-wait predator that gobbled up just about anything that passed by, including luckless lizards, misfortunate mammals, and even day-old dinosaurs.

Today, however, it looks as if it might be snapping at more than it can chew. At 88 pounds (40 kg), a German shepherd is almost ten times as heavy as this frog. But our frog is not backing off. It has sharp teeth, powerful jaws, and a mouth almost 12 inches (30 cm) wide.

It probably won't make a very tasty meal anyway. It has shell-like armor on its back, which may have allowed it to burrow underground to cool down. Or maybe the armor acted as protection from dinosaurs—and if it worked with dinosaurs, it will probably work with passing German shepherds, too.

BEELZEBUFO
PRONOUNCED
Bee-el-zee-BOO-foe

LIVED
Madagascar,
70 million
years ago

LENGTH
16.1 inches (41 cm)

WEIGHT
10 pounds (4.5 kg)

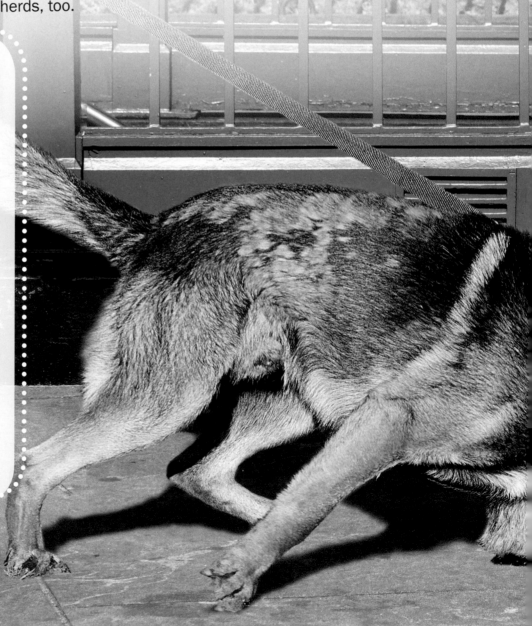

PAC-MAN FROGS

Living descendants of the devil frog are called Ceratophyrines. They have been nicknamed Pac-Man frogs, because their big mouth and round body shape resemble the 1980s video-game character.

New York City Transit

Su

New

FDNY
STREET TO STATION
COMMUNICATIONS

BROOKLYN BRIDGE STATION
A DIVISION IRT

MONSTER SNAKE
TITANOBOA

Something's hissssssing. And it's sssslipped through the water and sssssslithered into a pool where hippos are hanging out. Yes, it's a snake all right, but not just any snake. It's 48 feet (14.6 m) of pure muscle—longer than five ping-pong tables put end to end.

You wouldn't think a massive hippo would be troubled by a snake, no matter how big. But this is *Titanoboa*. It's going for the hippo's neck, ready to puncture the hide with its long, sharp teeth. And if you think that even *Titanoboa* would not be able to get its mouth around a hippo's neck, remember that a snake's lower jaws can unhinge into two halves.

Titanoboa's teeth were probably curved so that prey couldn't pull away. With its grip steady, it could then coil its immensely powerful body around the hippo. This would shut off the blood supply to the hippo's vital organs, such as its heart and brain. So *Titanoboa* would literally be squeezing the life out of this poor old hippo.

TITANOBOA
PRONOUNCED
Tie-tan-oh-BO-ah

LIVED
South America,
60–58 million years
ago

LENGTH
Up to 48 feet (14.6 m)

WEIGHT
About 1.25 tons
(1.13 metric tons)

WALKING JAWS

Titanoboa's jaws not only came apart but could move forward separately. So it would have "walked" its jaws along the body of the hippo to swallow it. Its curved teeth could grip on one side, while the other half of the jaw walked forward, until the whole hippo vanished!

DISSOLVED BY ACID

Once the hippo had been swallowed by *Titanoboa*, it would be dissolved by acids in the snake's stomach. The actual kill might take a matter of minutes, but the digestion would take days!

TERROR BIRD
PHORUSRHACID

This race has an unexpected entrant. Scientists call it a *phorusrhacid* but, as that is quite hard to pronounce, it's often called a "terror bird." And you can see why. With a massive head, long, powerful legs, and fearsome talons, the terror bird was a bit like a smaller version of *T. rex*. So you can be sure it has not come along for the ride—it's here for the riders! And chances are that it will get one.

How do we know terror birds were ferocious meat-eaters? One important clue is that their beaks curved downwards into a hook-like tip. Every living bird of prey has a beak like this for tearing off flesh—so it's a clear sign that terror birds also had a taste for meat. Indeed, the terror birds' hooks were so big that scientists think they were used to strike down repeatedly on prey with quick stabbing motions. The beak could be up to 18 in (46 cm) long and some birds grew 8–10 feet (2.5–3 m) tall—so it would be a bit like someone standing over you, hitting you with a hatchet!

PHORUSRHACID
PRONOUNCED
FOR-uss-RAY-kid

LIVED
South and
North America,
60–2 million
years ago

HEIGHT
Up to about 10 feet
(3 m)

WEIGHT
Up to 550 pounds
(250 kg)

UP TO SPEED

If you think the bird here would not keep up with the horses, think again. The fastest racehorse ran at 44 miles (70.76 km) per hour. Some scientists estimate that *Mesembriornis*, a 5-foot (1.5-m) terror bird, galloped along at 60 miles (97 km) per hour.

WALKING WHALE

AMBULOCETUS

Can you imagine an animal that swam like a whale but could also walk on dry land? Well, meet *Ambulocetus*. It's the big-headed animal on the right of the picture here.

On the left, a crocodile has just got a wildebeest by the neck—it is in the middle of killing it with its death roll. But it might have to endure a death roll of its own from *Ambulocetus*. Looks like a double dish of crocodile and wildebeest today for this prehistoric predator.

So how on earth did the strange-looking *Ambulocetus* come about? Around 50 million years ago, mammals were built for life on solid ground, but some started to evolve into sea creatures. Why? Probably because food was scarce on land and the sea was full of tasty treats: fish and crustaceans, such as crabs, lobsters, and crayfish. One of the first to do this was *Ambulocetus*. It could walk on land but was also at home in the water—as this croc is about to find out!

AMBULOCETUS
PRONOUNCED
Am-bew-low-SEE-tuss

LIVED
Shores of India,
50–48 million
years ago

LENGTH
About 10 feet (3 m)

WEIGHT
440–660 pounds
(200–300 kg)

GOOD VIBRATIONS

Ambulocetus probably picked up sound vibrations both in and out of the water through its lower jawbone. These sounds passed up to the inner ear. This is how modern predatory whales hear—they have no external part of the ear.

SPEEDY SWIMMER

Ambulocetus swam by arching its spine and pushing its lower body up and down in the water, like an otter or a whale. Powerful kicks with its back legs, which probably had webbed toes, gave the animal extra speed.

BONE CRUNCHER
ANDREWSARCHUS

In Asia, the tiger is the apex predator. This means no other animal preys on it. Big tigers can measure 10 feet (3 m) and have skulls 13 inches (35 cm) long. Well, here the tiger has more than met its match—it's the monster *Andrewsarchus*.

Scientists have only ever found one skull of *Andrewsarchus*, but it is more than double the length of a tiger's. The size of the body is anyone's guess, but if it were in the same proportion as a tiger, it would be more than 26 feet (8 m) long! Scientists don't think *Andrewsarchus* would have reached these lengths—but they are pretty sure it was the largest carnivorous land mammal ever. The size of the cheekbones tell us the jaws would have had immensely powerful muscles. These muscles, along with huge canines, would have been perfect for delivering a fatal bite to another animal's skull.

So, although they say don't catch a tiger by the tail, this *Andrewsarchus* shouldn't be too worried. After all, he is the apex predator here.

ANDREWSARCHUS
PRONOUNCED
Ann-droo-SAR-kuss

LIVED
Central Asia,
48–41 million
years ago

SKULL LENGTH
32 inches (83 cm);
width 22 inches (56 cm)

DINNER MENU

What did *Andrewsarchus* eat? Some scientists have suggested turtles because the only *Andrewsarchus* fossil to be found was in a prehistoric coastal area. But they could also have eaten giant herbivorous mammals, such as the rhino-like *Brontotherium*.

SNAPPING JAWS

HYAENODON

Feel like a nice relaxing day at the beach? A little sunbathing, swimming, and—er ... escaping from a *Hyaenodon*. This creature was one of the first big carnivorous mammals. It had massive jaws supported by extra muscles in its neck—and it used them to crush animal skulls. We know this because a fossil of an early type of cat called *Dinictis* has holes in its skull that match the tooth pattern of *Hyaenodon*. What's more, fossilized *Hyaenodon* waste contains pieces of animal skull.

Hyaenodon did not rely just on crushing animals in its jaws. It also had slicing teeth at the back of those jaws. As the animal grew older, the slicing teeth would grind against each other, keeping them sharp. As a result, *Hyaenodon* could eat smaller pieces rather than gulping down large chunks, which would have helped with digestion. To avoid being chewed up into very small pieces, these beachgoers need to get up that lifeguard tower. It's a very appropriately named tower, if you think about it.

HYAENODON
PRONOUNCED
Hi-EE-noh-don

LIVED
Plains of
North America,
Europe, Asia
and Africa,
40–20 million
years ago

LENGTH
Just over 10 feet (3 m)
(the largest species,
Hyaenodon gigas)

NO DOGS

RIVAL PREDATORS

Why did *Hyaenodon* die out? It might have had more competition from "bear dogs," such as *Amphicyon*. These were as lethal as *Hyaenodon* but probably faster, so they were better able to catch scurrying herbivores.

KILLER PIGS
ENTELODONTS

You've heard of foxes raiding a chicken shed and dogs chasing sheep in fields. But a pig terrorizing a farm? That couldn't happen. Oh yes it could, if the pig in question is an entelodont. They certainly want more than a few roots and grains on their dinner menu.

Entelodonts are often simply referred to as killer pigs. And here's why: they were massive creatures, at least twice the size of today's pigs. Their huge skulls had jaws and muscles designed for bone crushing. Fossils of primitive rhinos and camels have been found with wounds that were made by entelodonts.

They would even attack their fellow entelodonts. Many entelodont skulls have severe gashes up to 0.8 inches (2 cm) deep, which can only have been inflicted by other killer pigs. From studying these wounds, scientists can tell it was common for one pig to have its rival's head entirely in its mouth!

So this rancher should get out of that barn as quickly as possible. And if the entelodont wants to stay the night, let it!

ENTELODONT
PRONOUNCED
en-TELL-oh-dont

LIVED
North America,
Europe and Asia,
37–16 million
years ago

LENGTH
Up to 11 feet (3.5 m)

WEIGHT
About 930 pounds
(420 kg)

BIG HEAD

Daeodon was one of the largest entelodonts. It lived about 20 million years ago, and its skull was about 3 feet (90 cm) long—that's slightly bigger than a standard oil drum!

BIG BEAST IN THE BIG APPLE
PARACERATHERIUM

OK, what's the world's largest land mammal? An elephant? That's right if we are talking about the modern world. But the largest land mammal of all time was *Paraceratherium*. It weighed four times more than an African elephant and was twice as tall. And it looks like it's just come back from the dead!

Don't worry, no one's directly in danger here. *Paraceratherium* was an herbivore and it's probably looking for a park with a few trees to snack on. The pedestrians just need to make sure they don't get caught under its feet because it doesn't look like the nimblest of creatures. For the best (and safest) view, they probably should go inside a building—preferably three flights up for a great face-to-face encounter!

Paraceratherium is closely related to the rhino, but it lived like a giraffe, using its great height to feed on the tasty leaves out of reach of other animals. Scientists think it used its big incisor teeth to hold the branches and its big muscular lips to rip off the leaves.

PARACERATHERIUM
PRONOUNCED
Para-sera-THEE-rium
LIVED
Asia, 34–23 million years ago
HEIGHT
16 feet (5 m), at the shoulder
LENGTH
26 feet (8 m)
WEIGHT
16.5–22 tons (15–20 metric tons)

HEAVIEST MAMMAL

Paraceratherium might be the heaviest ever land mammal, but it can't compare with the blue whale, the heaviest mammal of all. At about 200 tons (180 metric tons), the blue whale is ten times heavier—and it is still around today, despite being hunted almost to extinction in the 20th century.

GIANT TOOTH
MEGALODON

In today's world, killer whales are the undisputed rulers of the oceans. They don't fear anyone—even great white sharks get taken out by killer whales. It's not hard to see why. They can grow up to 33 feet (10 m) long and weigh a whopping 11 US tons (10 metrictons). And their teeth can measure up to 4 inches (10 cm). This unfortunate sea lion is going to feel them . . . unless the killer whale feels *Megalodon*'s teeth first!

Megalodon was the biggest shark ever, about 40 times heavier than a great white. Its teeth were razor-sharp and serrated like steak knives. What's more, they were 7 inches (18 cm) long. Compare that with the great white's, which are only 1.2 inches (3 cm). Not surprising then, that *Megalodon* means "giant tooth" in Greek.

MEGALODON
PRONOUNCED
MEG-ah-low-don

LIVED
Oceans worldwide,
25–2.6 million years
ago

LENGTH
About 52 feet (16 m)

WEIGHT
Up to 110 tons
(100 metric tons)

STONE TONGUES
Before people understood what fossils were, it was thought that *Megalodon* teeth were the tips of dragons' tongues. But in 1667, Nicholas Steno, the Duke of Florence's physician, realized that they came from an extinct shark.

CAR CRUSHER!
It wasn't just the size of its teeth that made *Megalodon* so fearsome. It was the force with which it used them. In 2012, scientists estimated its bite was more than three times more powerful than that of *Tyrannosaurus rex* and almost 50 times more than a lion's— enough to crush a small car or a killer whale.

A WHALE OF A TIME

LIVYATAN

Wow, the fishermen on this boat have a front-row view of some amazing action! The ginormous creature is *Livyatan*, the biggest predatory whale ever known. It lived about 12 million years ago and probably ate almost anything that came its way—other whales, as well as dolphins, porpoises, sharks, sea turtles, seals, and seabirds, have been found at the site where the remains of *Livyatan* have been excavated. One thing is certain: it needed a lot food to keep its 50-foot (15-m) body going.

Scientists think it may have attacked from below, approaching from the murky depths and slamming into its target from underneath like a rocket fired from the sea floor. This has been called the Polaris attack, named after the submarine-launched missile. And it's worked here because it has successfully nabbed a hammerhead shark. Now the fishermen have to hope that it doesn't land on their boat!

LIVYATAN
PRONOUNCED
Li-VIE-ah-tan

LIVED
Shores of
South America,
13–12 million years ago

LENGTH
About 50 feet (15 m);
skull 10 feet (3 m) long

HUGE TEETH

Livyatan is related to modern sperm whales, which roam the oceans looking for giant squid to eat. However, today's sperm whale is a pussycat in comparison. It has small teeth and feeds by opening its jaws quickly so its prey is sucked into its mouth. *Livyatan*'s mouth was full of huge teeth, and, as you can see, it snatched its prey with a powerful bite, inflicting deep wounds, then tearing off flesh.

TITANIC TURTLE
STUPENDEMYS

You'd probably think that the massive turtle *Stupendemys* would have been safe from predators 10 million years ago, when it lived in the waters of what became the Amazon River. Surely no other animal would have taken on this Titan with its supersize, shield-like shell. But *Stupendemys* lived at the same time as some of the biggest crocodiles ever to lurk in Earth's watery places. *Purusaurus*, for instance, could grow to a massive 42 feet (13 m) long, weighed around 9 tons (8.5 metric tons), and probably would have made short work of *Stupendemys*.

However, *Stupendemys* doesn't have much to worry about here in the Everglades of Florida. It can take a relaxing dip in the swamp waters safe in the knowledge that even the largest alligators, at 13 feet (4 m), are not going do much damage to that shell.

STUPENDEMYS
PRONOUNCED
Stoo-PEND-ee-miss

LIVED
Northern South America, 10–5 million years ago

SHELL LENGTH
About 10 ft x 6 ft 6 in
(3 x 2 m)

WEIGHT
About 1.6 tons
(1.5 metric tons)

UNDERWATER EATER

Stupendemys wasn't the only giant turtle to prowl around the Amazon in days gone by. *Carbonemys* lived about 50 million years earlier, its shell was about 5 ft 6 in (1.7 m) long, and it had powerful jaws that could eat small crocodiles.

60

BEETLE ON A TURTLE

Stupendemys was so large, you could easily have placed a Volkswagen Beetle on its shell. The animal was so heavy that scientists think it was probably a poor swimmer and spent most of its time chilling underwater grazing on plants.

HUMONGOUS HEDGEHOG
DEINOGALERIX

In several parts of the world, including Britain, hedgehogs are becoming rarer and rarer. So if you found one while raking a pile of leaves, you'd probably be quite pleased to see it.

You might not feel the same way if you found *Deinogalerix*. This hedgehog was as big as a dog. And it looked truly bizarre. For a start, it did not have quills. What's more, it had a long, thin, cone-shaped head, small pointy ears and an exceptionally long tail. There is nothing to worry about, though. Scientists think this curious creature mainly ate invertebrates – small animals without backbones – such as beetles, dragonflies, crickets and possibly even snails. Some of the larger species, like this one, may have also hunted small mammals, reptiles and birds.

DEINOGALERIX
PRONOUNCED
Dye-no-GAL-eriks

LIVED
Gargano, Italy,
10–5 million years ago

LENGTH
Up to 60 cm (2 ft)

WEIGHT
Up to 4 kg (10 lb)

ISLAND LIFE

How did this hedgehog get so big? *Deinogalerix* lived on what was then an island and is now the Gargano region of Italy. Island species sometimes grow much larger than their mainland relatives because they often don't have many competitors for food and are not preyed on by large animals.

MONKEY BUSINESS
GIGANTOPITHECUS

Who is this unexpected visitor to the Great Wall of China? Meet *Gigantopithecus*, the biggest ape ever to walk the Earth. It's twice the height of a gorilla and three times its weight—but, even so, it's not a danger to the sightseers. By studying its teeth and jaws, scientists have discovered that *Gigantopithecus* liked a diet of fruit, nuts, and shoots. Some scientists think it might have gobbled up the occasional small mammal or lizard but only as a side dish.

Although *Gigantopithecus* might look like a gorilla, its closest living relative is actually the orangutan. Like the orangutan, it lived in forests—but its food became much harder to find when, around 100,000 years ago, the climate began to get cooler and forests started shrinking. And of course, unlike the orangutan, *Gigantopithecus* would have missed out on all the fruit growing in the treetops. It might be able to climb the Great Wall of China, but it was far too heavy to climb trees!

GIGANTOPITHECUS
PRONOUNCED
Jye-GAN-toe-PITH-
eh-kuss

LIVED
China, India,
Vietnam and Nepal,
9 million–100,000
years ago

LENGTH
10 feet (3 m)

WEIGHT
1,190 pounds
(540 kg)

MYSTERY BEAST
Scientists have found more than 1,000 fossilized teeth of *Gigantopithecus* and some of its jaw bones—but no fossils of its lower body. So no one is exactly sure what this beast looked like.

TOWERING CAMEL
TITANOTYLOPUS

There is only one winner in this camel race and it's the giant camel *Titanotylopus*. Just look at those legs go. *Titanotylopus* is twice the height of modern camels and the legs alone are taller than the jockey. There are a few questions you have to ask about this race, though. For a start, how did the jockey get on *Titanotylopus*? A stepladder? And, more importantly, how will he manage to stay on? It looks like it's going to be a bumpy ride!

Titanotylopus remains have been found across the United States, including Texas, Kansas, and Arizona. But giant camel fossils have also been found in the Arctic! Yes, that's right—about 3.4 million years ago, camels lived on Ellesmere Island in Canada, opposite Greenland, one of the world's coldest, bleakest spots. This camel—known as the High Arctic camel—wasn't as big as *Titanotylopus,* but it was still bigger by a third than today's camels.

TITANOTYLOPUS
PRONOUNCED
Tie-tan-oh-TIE-low-puss

LIVED
Plains of North America, Europe and Asia.
5 million-300,000 years ago

LENGTH
13 feet (4m)

WEIGHT
1.1-2.2 tons
(1-2 metric tons)

ARCTIC DRIFTER
The High Arctic camel was well-adapted for life in the cold. Its wide, flat feet enabled it to walk on snow, and as in the desert, it could live off energy stored in its hump.

KING OF THE GRASSLANDS
MAMMOTH

This is what we call a real stand-off: monster fire truck versus, er, monster. This is a Steppe mammoth, the largest mammoth that ever existed. It weighed twice as much as the largest elephant of today and its tusks were 16 feet (5 m) long.

You think this stand-off is just fantasy? Don't be so sure. In May 2013, on the island of Maly Lyakhovsky, north of Russia, a mammoth was found buried in the frozen ground. It had been eaten alive by wolves while stuck in a peat bog. Despite this grisly attack, most of its body parts were intact—including three legs, most of its body, and even its trunk. Its blood had also frozen—and from this, scientists are hoping to get DNA to clone a new mammoth. So maybe, in the future, the world really will be like the movie *Jurassic Park*, and stand-offs like this will be an everyday happening.

MAMMOTH
LIVED
Europe and Asia,
5 million years ago–
1,650 BCE

SHOULDER HEIGHT
Up to 13 feet (4 m)

WEIGHT
11–16.5 tons
(10–15 metric tons)

FIRE RESCUE

DIAL 911

END OF AN ERA

Why did mammoths die out? Some scientists think that when the Ice Age ended, around 12,000 years ago, mammoths lost their habitat, as open grasslands and woodlands were replaced by forests. Others think the animals were hunted to extinction by humans. Perhaps both these factors, combined with rising sea levels, brought about the end of these majestic beasts.

ENGINE

MIGHTY RODENT
JOSEPHOARTIGASIA

The capybara is a large rodent that can grow up to 1.34 m (4 ft 4 in) long. Fortunately you're unlikely to meet it beause it lives in the Amazon rainforests. Now can you imagine a capybara relative as big as a buffalo—the largest rodent ever? It went by the name of *Josephoartigasia* and it used its huge incisor teeth with the same bite force as a tiger. It's simply the last thing you'd want to see in the garden . . .

At the moment at least, these *Josephoartigasia* seem happy rooting around the trash and having a relaxing swim in the pool.
But it won't be long before they are inside the house. Rodents can chew their way through brick, wood, cinder blocks, concrete, and even a 0.4-inch (1-cm) thick sheet of metal. So just imagine how easily *Josephoartigasia* could break into a house with those incisors!

JOSEPHOARTIGASIA
PRONOUNCED
Joe-SEPH-oh-artig-AH-see-ah

LIVED
South America,
4–2 million years ago

LENGTH
10 feet (3 m)

WEIGHT
2,200 pounds
(1,000 kg)

BIG HEAD
Josephoartigasia's skull was 20 inches (53 cm) long—much bigger than a lion's or tiger's. Its incisor teeth measured 12 inches (30 cm)—way longer than bananas!

GIANT BEAVERS
CASTOROIDES

Beavers are truly amazing creatures. They build dams on rivers to give protection from predators, such as coyotes, wolves, and bears, and to provide easy access to food. And in the middle of the still water created by the dam, they make lodges from sticks, mud, and rocks. Here, they sleep, eat, and bring up their young (known as kits).

Beavers are the architects, engineers, and landscape designers of the animal world. And they do all the hard work themselves. They drag logs along mudslides and float them along canals to put them in place. With their sharp incisor teeth, they can fell trees (3 feet 9 inches (1.15 m) in diameter.

And modern beavers are only 60–90 cm (2–3 ft) long. Now imagine what a beaver almost four times bigger could do. This dam is being built by giant beavers known as *Castoroides*. They lived in North America until about 10,000 years ago. It looks as if they are not satisfied with logs—you clearly need a car for a state-of-the-art dam.

CASTOROIDES
PRONOUNCED
Kass-tor-OY-deez

LIVED
Woodlands of
North America,
3 million–10,000 years
ago

LENGTH
Up to 8 feet (2.5 m)

WEIGHT
198–276 pounds
(90–125 kg)

BIG RODENTS

Castoroides is the largest rodent ever known in North America. The only rodents known to be bigger are *Phoberomys* and *Josephoartigasia* (see page 70), both of which lived in South America.

THE LIZARD OF AUS

MEGALANIA

Imagine getting home and finding this vicious creature looming over the porch! It's *Megalania*, the largest land-based lizard known. It lived in Australia until humans moved there some 50,000–40,000 years ago. And it probably ate the large marsupial mammals that roamed the Outback in those days. These included weighty wombats, such as *Diprotodon*, and colossal kangaroos, such as *Procoptodon*. At the same time, it would have had to look out for the marsupial lion *Thylacoleo* and the crocodile *Quinkana*, which lived on the land and was about the same size as *Megalania*.

This *Megalania* looks like it's after a meal. It smelt by flicking out its forked tongue, and here it can definitely tell there is something tasty inside the house. Scientists think it had venom glands loaded with deadly poison, just like modern Komodo dragons. So when *Megalania*'s teeth tore the flesh of its prey, it would also inject venom. This would paralyse the victim's muscles and stop the wound from healing. So a word of advice for everyone in that house: get inside and lock all the doors and windows!

MEGALANIA
PRONOUNCED
Meg-ah-LANE-ee-ah
LIVED
South-eastern
Australia, 2
million–50,000 years
ago
LENGTH
18–23 feet (5.5–7 m)
WEIGHT
2.1 tons (1.94
metric tons)

STING IN THE TAIL

Megalania did not just use its tail to help it stand up, as here. Scientists think *Megalania*'s tail was also a lethal weapon for knocking out and injuring prey. The largest modern lizard, the Komodo dragon, uses its tail in exactly the same way.

SMALL WONDERS
DWARF ELEPHANTS

Can you imagine elephants that you can pat on the head like a dog? No, we are not talking baby elephants. These are dwarf elephants, which grew to only about 39 inches (1 m) tall. Until about 10,000 years ago, they lived on islands in the Mediterranean Sea, including Cyprus, Malta, Crete, Sicily, and Sardinia.

So how did they arrive on these islands? Well, the climate has changed a lot in the last 2–3 million years, and this has caused sea levels to vary. When sea levels were low, elephants could reach the islands from Africa and Asia. Once sea levels rose again, though, they would often be stranded there.

OK, but how did the elephants get so small and—let's face it—cute? Perhaps only the small elephants survived when drought hit the islands. Also, there was no need for elephants to be large. In Africa, the elephant's huge size puts off lions and other predators from attacking them. But on the islands there were no big predators. There are not many predators in this field, either. The dwarf elephants seem to feel at home here, enjoying life with a flock of sheep.

DWARF ELEPHANTS
LIVED
Islands in the Mediterranean Sea, 2.5 million–10,000 years ago
LENGTH
5–7 feet 6 inches (1.5–2.3 m)
WEIGHT
400–500 pounds (180–225 kg)

BALANCING ACT
If you put one fully grown modern African elephant on one side of huge weighing scales, you would need about 10 dwarf elephants on the other side to balance it.

RUNAWAY RHINO
ELASMOTHERIUM

Every July charging bulls, led by human runners, are let loose on the streets of Pamplona in Spain. And yes, they cause complete havoc. Running at an average speed of 15 miles (24 km) per hour, the bulls usually injure between 50 and 100 people. Those who slip or are pushed over are the lucky ones—you just want to avoid being gored on those horns!

This year, things have become a whole lot more dangerous, because look what has joined the fun: an *Elasmotherium*. That's a giant rhino to you and me. These creatures were the size of elephants—about 4.4 tons (4 metric tons) of solid flesh, bone, and muscle. They were covered in hair, and scientists think they galloped like horses. What's more, while bulls' horns seem dangerous, check out *Elasmotherium*'s. Now the bulls might be in as much danger as the runners . . .

ELASMOTHERIUM
PRONOUNCED
Eh-laz-moe-THEE-ree-um

LIVED
Plains of Asia and Eastern Europe,
2 million–30,000 years ago

LENGTH
20 feet (6 m)

WEIGHT
3.3-4.4 tons
(3-4 metric tons)

HEIGHT
6 feet 6 inches (2 m)

MISSING HORNS

Elasmotherium's horn was made from keratin—the same substance that makes up human hair and fingernails. Unfortunately, this doesn't fossilize well, so nobody knows the exact length of the horn. But scientists think it was about 5 feet 9 inches (1.75 m) long.

LIVED WITH HUMANS

In 2016, new research on a piece of *Elasmotherium* skull found in Kazakhstan showed that the animal lived until about 30,000 years ago. Previously scientists thought it had died out 350,000 years ago. This means the creature lived at the same time as humans.

FANGTASTIC FELINE

SMILODON

We all know about the ferocity of modern lions, tigers, and leopards. Well, they are pussycats compared to the saber-toothed cats. These prehistoric predators were generally bigger and more powerfully built—and the largest of all was *Smilodon*. It had massively powerful front legs and fangtastic canines: they were 8 inches (20 cm) long and serrated on both edges.

Smilodon lived in North and South America and hunted bison, camels, and maybe even baby mammoths and giant sloths. Most of these animals don't live in the wild anymore. So these *Smilodon* have found other prey: a bear.

How did *Smilodon* capture its prey? There was probably no running involved. *Smilodon* was heavily built and had a very short tail, which meant its balance and agility would have been poor, unlike most modern big cats. So scientists think *Smilodon* had to be more cunning—it probably pounced on prey from trees or rocks. Then it would sink its canines into its victim's neck and wait until the wounded animal bled to death.

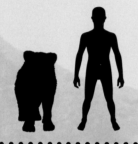

SMILODON
PRONOUNCED
SMY-loh-don

LIVED
North and
South America,
2 million–10,000 years
ago

LENGTH
6 feet (1.8 m)

WEIGHT
Up to 880 pounds
(400 kg)

COME TOGETHER
Scientists believe that *Smilodon* lived in packs. Why? Because fossils often show they had leg fractures that had healed. The only way they could have survived such injuries was if other members of a pack had brought them food.

GIANT SLOTH
MEGATHERIUM

Today's sloths live in trees in South America and weigh 13 pounds (6 kg) at most. That's less than a Jack Russell terrier. *Megatherium*, however, wouldn't last long in a tree—and the tree wouldn't last too long either! It weighs 4.4 tons (4 metric tons— about the same as an elephant!

As you can see, this giant sloth can reach leaves in the treetops simply by standing on its hind legs. In this position, it is the same height as a modern giraffe. To get at any leaves still out of reach, it could use its large claws and powerful arms to pull branches down to its mouth. Scientists think *Megatherium* also had a long, strong tongue that it wrapped around the branches to strip off leaves and fresh growth. And if there were no trees to feed on? Then it would use its big claws to dig at plant roots. And there are lots in this garden to try!

MEGATHERIUM
PRONOUNCED
Meg-ah-THEE-ree-um
LIVED
South America,
2 million–10,000 years
ago
LENGTH
20 feet (6 m)
WEIGHT
4.4 tons
(4 metric tons)

KILLER CLAWS?

Megatherium's huge claws measured almost 12 inches (30 cm) long and prevented it from putting its feet flat on the ground—it had to walk on the sides of its feet. Some scientists have even claimed that *Megatherium* used these claws to slash and kill other animals. They think it ate meat as well as plants.

CLIMB OR DIG?

Frenchman Georges Cuvier was the first to identify the giant sloth, in 1796. He thought its huge claws enabled it to climb trees. Then he changed his mind—probably when he realized it was too big to climb trees! He decided the sloth must have lived underground and used its claws to dig tunnels.

MAGNIFICENT MARSUPIAL

DIPROTODON

Looks like we have an extra player for the volleyball match. Not sure that this pigeon-toed creature is going to be the best teammate, though. It doesn't look like it can make the sharpest moves or react very quickly.

So who—or what—is this new player? It's a *Diprotodon*, and it lived in Australia until 40,000 years ago. Like the Australian kangaroo and koala, it was a marsupial, which means it kept its young in a pouch. Some people think *Diprotodon* looks a little like the koala. Perhaps, but only if you imagine the koala to be the size of a hippopotamus and fully capable of crunching a human skull between its two back molars! *Diprotodon* was a plant-eater—but hippos are also vegetarians, and that hasn't stopped them killing people. So maybe the players should take a time-out and chill with an ice cream until their court is *Diprotodon*-free!

DIPROTODON
PRONOUNCED
Dye-PRO-toe-don

LIVED
Australia,
1.8 million–40,000
years ago

LENGTH
Up to 13 feet (4m)

WEIGHT
Up to 3 tons
(3 metric tons)

Diprotodon's pouch faced backwards, so the baby's view of the world would have been framed by its mother's hind legs! The modern Australian wombat also has a backwards-facing pouch. When it burrows, soil doesn't get in the pouch!

RUFFLING FEATHERS
ELEPHANT BIRD

Anyone walking down this street had better watch out. They're going to bump into one of the biggest birds that ever existed. And it will do more than ruffle a few feathers. Those massively powerful legs can break bones and worse. But hey, at least it won't eat the passerby! Scientists believe it was a herbivore. This ostrich-like bird lived on the island of Madagascar and couldn't fly, but it grew so big because it had plenty of fruit to eat in the lush forests and no predators to bother it.

In fact, its only predator seems to have been humans. Scientists think humans hunted the bird to extinction in the 17th or 18th century. You can see why. Elephant birds' eggs were bigger than footballs and would have made an eggstraordinary 30 omelettes. And there would have been plenty of meat on the bird itself. It is sad to see such an imposing creature go. But scientists have been able to extract DNA from an elephant bird's egg, so maybe one day it will be seen walking down the road.

ELEPHANT BIRD

LIVED
Madagascar, from about 40,000 years ago until the 17th century

HEIGHT
Up to 10 feet (3 m)

WEIGHT
Up to 1,100 pounds (500 kg)

VERY EGGSPENSIVE
Intact elephant birds' eggs are very rare and valuable. In 2013, the London auctioneers Christie's sold an egg for a whopping $101,813 (£66,675). That turned out to be a cracking sale.

TIMELINE

CAMEROCERAS

Named after the Greek for "chambered horn"

Nautiloids get their name from the Greek "nautilos" for sailor. The Greek philosopher and scientist Aristotle was one of the first people to study nautiloids.

PLIOSAURUS FUNKEI

Named after the Greek for "more lizard" and Bjørn Funke who discovered it

Pliosaurs were massive reptiles that swam the Jurassic seas. There are five other known species of *Pliosaurus*.

ARTHROPLEURA

Named after the Greek for "jointed ribs"

Fossil hunters have found lots of preserved footprints of *Arthropleura*, as well as fossilized body parts. They show that the giant millipede moved quickly across forest floors, swerving to avoid trees and rocks.

DUNKLEOSTEUS

Named after its discoverer David Dunkle and *osteon,* the Greek for "bone"

Heavy *Dunkleosteus* was probably not a fast swimmer, so it probably went after slow prey or used ambush tactics.

INOSTRANCEVIA

Named after Russian geologist Alexandr Inostrantzev

The herbivore *Scutosaurus* was probably one of *Inostrancevia*'s main meals. It was massively built and heavily armored, but it could not have outrun *Inostrancevia*.

470 MILLION YEARS AGO

Around 230 million years ago: first dinosaurs evolve

SARCOSUCHUS

Named after the Greek for "flesh crocodile"

Sarcosuchus' long snout had a bowl-shaped ending called a bulla. Scientists are not sure what it was for. It may have helped the croc to smell or let it to make calls to fellow *Sarcosuchus*.

XIPHACTINUS

Named after the Latin and Greek for "sword ray"

Xiphactinus might have been a lethal predator, but it was also prey for larger fish. A fossil of the prehistoric shark *Cretoxyrhina* was found with scattered bones of *Xiphactinus* inside it.

BEELZEBUFO

Named after Beelzebub (the devil) and *bufo*, Latin for toad

Devil frog fossils were first found in 1993, but it took 15 years and 75 more fossils to work out what it looked like.

LEEDSICHTHYS

Named after Alfred Leeds and *ichthys*, the Greek for ish"

A tooth found in one *Leedsichthys* fossil proves that it was attacked, or at least scavenged after its death, by the vicious crocodile-like reptile *Metriorhynchus*.

QUETZALCOATLUS

Named after the Aztec flying serpent god, Quetzalcoatl

Most scientists think *Quetzalcoatlus* ate small animals on land, as a modern stork does. But others think it scavenged dead carcasses, such as a vulture, or skimmed up fish in its long beak like a seabird.

66 million years ago: end of the dinosaurs

STUPENDEMYS

Named after the Greek for "astonishing turle"

The earliest turtle evolved around 220 million years ago. When the dinosaurs died out about 66 million years ago, turtles survived because they could live on very little for a long time.

ANDREWSARCHUS

Named after naturalist Roy Chapman Andrews and the Greek, *archos*, for ruler

Andrewsarchus is widely considered to be the largest carnivorous land mammal ever. Today's largest is the polar bear.

LIVYATAN

Scientists originally called the creature Leviathan after the biblical sea monster. But they didn't realize a type of mammoth was already called Leviathan. So it is now often named *Livyatan*—the original Hebrew spelling. The species *Livyatan melvillei* refers to Herman Melville, author of the whaling novel *Moby-Dick*.

TITANOBOA

Meaning "titanic boa," or huge boa (a snake of the Boidae family)

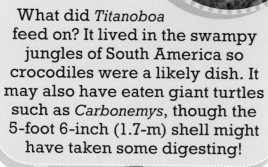

What did *Titanoboa* feed on? It lived in the swampy jungles of South America so crocodiles were a likely dish. It may also have eaten giant turtles such as *Carbonemys*, though the 5-foot 6-inch (1.7-m) shell might have taken some digesting!

PARACERATHERIUM

Named after the Greek for "near the hornless beast"

Paraceratherium, first discovered in 1907–1908, was named because it resembled *Aceratherium*, another rhino-like creature whose name means—yes, you guessed it—"hornless beast."

GIGANTOPITHECUS

Named after the Greek for "giant ape"

The first time that the existence of *Gigantopithecus* came to light was in 1935, when palaeontologist Ralph von Koenigswald found an extremely large fossilized molar tooth in an apothecary shop in Hong Kong! (The Chinese call old animal teeth dragons' teeth' and use them in traditional medicine.).

ELASMOTHERIUM

Named after the Greek for "thin plate beast"

When fossils from this giant, one-horned beast were first discovered in Siberia, they were thought to belong to the mythical unicorn. Stories were told of its horn being so large it had to be transported by sledge. *Elasmotherium* is still informally known as the Siberian unicorn.

SMILODON

Named after the Greek for "knife/saber tooth"

Saber-toothed cats evolved from the Carnivora group of mammals about 42 million years ago. Their acute senses made them excellent hunters. *Smilodon* was one of the last saber-toothed cats.

MEGATHERIUM

Named after the Greek for "great beast"

Megatherium tracks left on the ground—as well as its bones—have been fossilized. These prove that it walked on both two feet and all fours.

ELEPHANT BIRD

The elephant bird looks like an oversized ostrich, but its closest living relative is the chicken-sized kiwi of New Zealand, which is also flightless. The elephant bird—the heaviest bird ever—may have had a kiwi-like ancestor

UNCOVERING THE PAST

Without the careful work of palaeontologists (pronounced: pay-lee-en-tol-o-gist), we would know nothing about our prehistoric past. These scientists search for fossils, the remains of extinct animals, to identify and understand early life forms.

A body fossil is the actual part of an animal, such as teeth or bones, preserved in rock. Fossils of the same animal can be discovered in different places. Fossils of the largest land mammal *Paraceratherium* were first discovered in Balochistan, Pakistan, in 1907–08. Others have been found in Kazakhstan, China, and Mongolia.

Scientists use these fossilized remains to reconstruct the whole creature. If they are exceptionally lucky, they find complete skeletons to work from. But usually there are bones missing. The bones may have disintegrated or a predator might have eaten some bones of the animal it killed!

However, scientists can remake the whole animal by comparing its skeleton with other skeletons of the same animal. They often know where muscles were positioned too because the bones may have scars where the muscles were attached. Once they have an idea of the size of the muscles, they can estimate the animal's weight. Skin is rarely preserved, so scientists often disagree about its color and texture and if it had fur or feathers—all part of the fun of solving fossil jigsaw puzzles!

Anyone can find a fossil!

You don't need to be a professional palaeontologist to discover a prehistoric creature. Many have been found by children. In 2015, a young girl discovered the fossil of a 25-million-year-old flightless bird in Canada. It was a new species of Plotopterid, a group of penguin-like birds.

Perhaps the greatest fossil hunter of all was 12-year-old Mary Anning, who found the first complete skeleton of the marine reptile *Ichthyosaurus* in England in 1811. Begin your own searches by joining a fossil-hunting group or organization.

Fossil of a trilobite, a hard-shelled sea creature that lived over 520 million years ago

INDEX

The Author

Matthew Rake lives in London, UK, and has worked in publishing for more than 20 years. He has written on a wide variety of topics for adults as well as children, including science, sports, and the arts.

The Artist

Award-winning illustrator Simon Mendez combines his love of nature and drawing by working as an illustrator with a focus on scientific and natural subjects. He paints on many themes but mainly concentrates on portraits and animal subjects. He lives in the United Kingdom.